CW00517099

THE KETO DIET COOKBOOK

FOR WOMEN OVER 50

LUNCH RECIPES

Quick, Easy and Delicious Low Carb Recipes to keep
your weight under control and burn fat

Debbie McDowell

Copyright © 2021 by Debbie McDowell

TABLE OF CONTENTS

KETO DIET OVER 50: LUNCH RECIPES

Spare Ribs

Preparation time: 10 minutes

Cooking time: 8 hours

Servings: 6

Ingredients:

- ✓ 1-pound pork loin ribs
- ✓ 1 teaspoon olive oil
- ✓ 1 teaspoon minced garlic ;1/4 teaspoon cumin
- ✓ 1/4 teaspoon chili powder
- ✓ 1 tablespoon butter
- ✓ 1 tablespoons water

Directions:

- ➢ Mix the olive oil, minced garlic, cumin, and chili flakes in a bowl.
- ➢ Melt the butter and add to the spice mixture.
- ➢ Stir it well and add water. Stir again.
- ➢ Then rub the pork ribs with the spice mixture generously and place the ribs in the slow cooker.

➢ Close the lid and cook the ribs for 8 hours on Low.

➢ When the ribs are cooked, serve them immediately!

Nutrition: Calories 203, Fat 14.1, Fiber 0.6, Carbs 10, Protein 9.8

Pork Shoulder

Preparation time: 25 minutes

Cooking time: 7 hours

Servings: 6

Ingredients:

- ✓ 1-pound pork shoulder
- ✓ 2 cups water
- ✓ 1 onion, peeled
- ✓ 2 garlic cloves, peeled
- ✓ 1 teaspoon peppercorns
- ✓ 1 teaspoon chili flakes
- ✓ 1/2 teaspoon paprika
- ✓ 1 teaspoon turmeric
- ✓ 1 teaspoon cumin

Directions:

- ➢ Sprinkle the pork shoulder with the peppercorns, chili flakes, paprika, turmeric, and cumin.
- ➢ Stir it well and let it sit for 15 minutes to marinate.
- ➢ Transfer the pork shoulder to the slow cooker.
- ➢ Add water and peeled the onion.
- ➢ Add garlic cloves and close the lid.
- ➢ Cook the pork shoulder for 7 hours on Low.

➢ Remove the pork shoulder from the slow cooker and serve!

Nutrition: Calories 234, Fat 16.4, Fiber 0.7, Carbs 2.8, Protein 18

Lamb Chops

Preparation time: 15 minutes

Cooking time: 3 hours

Servings: 2

Ingredients:

- ✓ 1oz. lamb chops
- ✓ 1 tablespoon tomato puree
- ✓ 1/2 teaspoon cumin
- ✓ 1/2 teaspoon ground coriander
- ✓ 1 teaspoon garlic powder
- ✓ 1 teaspoon butter ;1tablespoons water

Directions:

- ➤ Mix the tomato puree, cumin, ground coriander, garlic powder, and water in the bowl.
- ➤ Brush the lamb chops with the tomato puree mixture on each side and let marinate for 20 minutes.
- ➤ Toss the butter in the slow cooker.
- ➤ Add the lamb chops and close the lid.
- ➤ Cook the lamb chops for 3 hours on High.
- ➤ Transfer the cooked lamb onto serving plates and enjoy!

Nutrition: Calories 290, Fat 12.5, Fiber 0.4, Carbs 2, Protein 40.3

Rosemary Leg of Lamb

Preparation time: 15 minutes

Cooking time: 7 hours

Servings: 8

Ingredients:

- ✓ 2-pound leg of lamb
- ✓ 1 onion 2 cups water
- ✓ 1 garlic clove, peeled
- ✓ 1 tablespoon mustard seeds
- ✓ 1 teaspoon salt
- ✓ 1/2 teaspoon turmeric
- ✓ 1 teaspoon ground black pepper

Directions:

- ➢ Chop the garlic clove and combine it with the mustard seeds, turmeric, black pepper, and salt.
- ➢ Peel the onion and grate it.
- ➢ Mix the grated onion and spice mixture.
- ➢ Rub the leg of lamb with the grated onion mixture.
- ➢ Put the leg of lamb in the slow cooker and cook it for 7 hours on Low.
- ➢ Serve the cooked meal!

Nutrition: Calories 225, Fat 8.7, Fiber 0.6, Carbs 2.2, Protein 32.4

Creamy Chicken Thighs

Preparation time: 15 minutes

Cooking time: 6 hours

Servings: 4

Ingredients:

- ✓ 1-pound chicken thighs, skinless
- ✓ 1/4 cup almond milk, unsweetened
- ✓ 1 tablespoon full-fat cream cheese
- ✓ 1 teaspoon salt
- ✓ 1 onion, diced
- ✓ 1 teaspoon paprika

Directions

- ➢ Mix the almond milk and full-fat cream.
- ➢ Add salt, diced onion, and paprika.
- ➢ Stir the mixture well.
- ➢ Place the chicken thighs in the slow cooker.
- ➢ Add the almond milk mixture and stir it gently.
- ➢ Close the slow cooker lid and cook the chicken thighs for 6 hours on High.
- ➢ Transfer the cooked chicken thighs into the serving bowls and serve immediately!

Nutrition: Calories 224, Fat 14.3, Fiber 1.1, Carbs 4.7, Protein 18.9

Jerk Chicken

Preparation time: 25 minutes

Cooking time: 5 hours

Servings: 4

Ingredients:

- ➤ 1 teaspoon nutmeg
- ➤ 1 teaspoon cinnamon
- ➤ 1 teaspoon minced garlic ;1/2 teaspoon cloves
- ➤ 1 teaspoon ground coriander
- ➤ 1 tablespoon Erythritol
- ➤ 1-pound chicken thighs
- ➤ 1/2 cup water
- ➤ 1 tablespoon butter

Directions:

- ➤ Mix the nutmeg, cinnamon, minced garlic, cloves, and ground coriander.
- ➤ Add Erythritol and stir the ingredients until well blended.
- ➤ Sprinkle the chicken thighs with the spice mixture.
- ➤ Let the chicken thighs sit for 10 minutes to marinate, then put the chicken thighs in the slow cooker.
- ➤ Add the butter and water.

> ➢ Close the lid and cook Jerk chicken for 5 hours on Low.

> ➢ Serve Jerk chicken immediately!

Nutrition: Calories 247, Fat 11.5, Fiber 0.5, Carbs 4.9, Protein 33

Slow Cooker Lemon and Olive Chicken

Preparation Time: 15 min

Cooking time: 6 hrs.

Serves: 8

Ingredients

- ➢ 2 chopped carrots,
- ➢ 2 chopped ribs celery,
- ➢ 1 chopped bulb. fennel
- ➢ 1 chopped onion,
- ➢ 16 green olives stuffed
- ➢ 4 cloves crushed garlic,
- ➢ bay leaves
- ➢ 1/2 tsp. oregano
- ➢ 1/4 tsp. of salt
- ➢ 1/4 tsp. of pepper
- ➢ 12 chicken thighs
- ➢ 3/4 cup chicken broth
- ➢ 1/4 cup white flour
- ➢ 2 tbsp. of lemon juice
- ➢ 1/2 cup fresh parsley chopped
- ➢ Grated zest 1 Lemon

Directions:

- ➢ Combine carrots, celery, fennel, onion, olives, garlic, and spices in a cooker. Place chicken pieces on vegetable top, then add water and broth and cook. Whisk one cup flour and lemon juice in broth and cook till thickened. Sprinkle parsley in the end and serve hot.

➤ Enjoy!

Nutrition: Calories 278 Fat 11 Fiber,: 7 Carbs 4, Protein 21

Crock-Pot Whole Chicken Recipe with Garlic Herb Butter

Preparation Time: 15 min

Cooking time: 3 hrs.

Servings: 6

Ingredients

➢ 4 sprigs rosemary

➢ 12 sprigs thyme

➢ 6 tbsp. soft butter

➢ 1 garlic head

➢ 2 tsp. parsley

➢ 2 tsp. of sea salt

➢ 1/2 tsp. of paprika

➢ 1/2 tsp. of black pepper

➢ 5-lb. chicken

➢ 1 large chopped yellow onion

Directions:

➢ Mash butter, garlic, and spices in a bowl. Grease cooker with butter and put a layer of onions in it. Then place chicken on onions and rub spiced butter over that chicken. Cook for 5-8 hours on Low.

➢ **Nutrition: Calories 156, Fat 12 Fiber: 3, Carbs 3, Protein 24**

Healthy Slow Cooker Chicken Cacciatore

Preparation Time: 10 min

Cooking Time: 3 hrs.

Servings: 4

Ingredients

- ➢ 2 minced garlic cloves
- ➢ 1/2 large diced onion
- ➢ 1 large diced bell pepper
- ➢ 14.5 oz. drained diced canned tomatoes
- ➢ 1 tbsp. rosemary
- ➢ 1 tbsp. thyme
- ➢ 4 chicken breasts
- ➢ 1 tsp. of sea salt
- ➢ 1/4 tsp. of black pepper
- ➢ bay leaf

Directions:

- ➢ Season the chicken breasts on both sides with salt and pepper and place it in the cooker.
- ➢ Combine all vegetables and spices in a bowl and pour sauce evenly over the chicken. Cook for 3 to 4 hours on high or 6 to 8 hours on low flame.

Nutrition: Calories 378, Fat 13 Fiber: 3, Carbs 2, Protein 24

Crock-Pot Slow Cooker Crack Chicken

Preparation Time: 10 min

Cooking Time: 3 hrs.

Servings: 10

Ingredients

- 2 lb. of chicken breast
- 2 tbsp. parsley
- 1 tbsp. dill
- 1 tbsp. chives
- 1 tsp. powdered garlic
- 1 tsp. powdered onion powder
- 1/2 tsp. of black pepper
- 16 oz. pieces cream cheese
- 1 cup shredded cheddar cheese
- 1/2 cup cooked bacon bits
- 1/3 cup chopped green onions

Directions:

- Place the chicken in the cooker and sprinkle herbs and spices. Arrange cream cheese pieces over the chicken and cook for 3-4 hours on high or 6-8 hours on low until the chicken is easy to shred.

Nutrition: Calories 156, Fat 9 Fiber: 6, Carbs 2.1, Protein 21

Keto Low Carb Pot Roast Slow Cooker

Preparation Time: 15 min

Cooking Time: 10 hrs.

Servings: 12

Ingredients

- 4 lb. of chuck roast
- 4 tsp. of sea salt
- 1 tsp. of black pepper
- 2 tbsp. of avocado oil
- 1 1/2 cup chopped radishes
- 1 1/2 cup sliced carrots
- 1/2 large chopped onion
- 3 sprigs rosemary
- 4-5 sprigs thyme
- 2 cups any broth

Directions:

- Marinate chuck roast with salt and black pepper for 30 to 45 minutes. Meanwhile, brown onions, radishes, and carrots. Add chuck roast, veggies, and beef broth in the greased slow cooker. Add seasoning. Cook for 10-12 hours on low flame till tender.

Nutrition: Calories 365, Fat 11 Fiber: 6, Carbs 2.1, Protein 12

Slow Cooker Garlic Parmesan Chicken Wings

Preparation Time: 20 min

Cooking Time: 3 hrs.

Servings: 8

Ingredients

➢ 4 lb. of chicken wings

➢ 1 tsp. of sea salt

➢ 1/4 tsp. of black pepper

➢ 1/2 cup melted butter

➢ 6 cloves minced garlic

➢ 1 cup shredded parmesan cheese

Directions:

➢ Marinate chicken with salt and pepper. Sauté garlic for a minute spread it on chicken wings. Cook wings for 3 hours. Broil wings in the oven for about 5 minutes on each side, until crispy and golden. Top with shredded parmesan cheese. Return to the oven for 1-2 minutes until melted.

Nutrition: Calories 267, Fat 21 Fiber: 6, Carbs 3, Protein 12

Crock Pot Creamy Tuscan Garlic Chicken

Preparation Time: 15 min

Cooking Time: 3 hrs.

Servings: 4

Ingredients

- ➢ 1 tbsp. of olive oil
- ➢ 6 cloves minced garlic; 1 cup of heavy cream
- ➢ 1/3 cup of chicken broth
- ➢ 3/4 cup parmesan cheese grated
- ➢ 4 chicken breasts
- ➢ 1 tbsp. of Italian seasoning
- ➢ sea salt black pepper
- ➢ 1/2 cup sun-dried chopped tomatoes
- ➢ 2 cup chopped spinach

Directions:

- ➢ Sauté garlic for one minute, add cream and chicken broth, let it simmer for ten minutes, then combine it with parmesan cheese. Meanwhile, add seasoning to the chicken and cook. Add prepared sauce to chicken and cook for 3-4 hours. Add chopped spinach for few minutes. Spoon the liquid over the chicken before serving.

Nutrition: Calories 254, Fat 11 Fiber: 4, Carbs 2, Protein 24

Keto Nachos - Slow Cooker Chicken Low Carb Nachos

Preparation Time: 5 min

Cooking Time: 8 Hrs.

Servings: 4

Ingredients

- cheddar cheese
- 16 oz. salsa verde jar
- 4 chicken breasts
- 1 tomato
- sour cream
- salsa
- shredded cheese
- green onion

Directions:

- Place the chicken breasts in your slow cooker. Pour salsa verde over chicken and cook for 2 hours. Prepare the cheddar cheese chips according to the recipe. Top the chips with the shredded chicken and your favorite nacho toppings.

Nutrition: Calories 248, Fat 9 Fiber: 8, Carbs 1.9, Protein 29

Keto Chicken Pot Pie

Preparation Time: 42 min

Cooking Time: 3 hrs.

Servings: 8 servings

Ingredients

- For the Chicken Pot Pie Filling:
- 2 tbsp. butter
- 1/2 cup of mixed veggies
- 1/4 onion diced
- 1/4 tsp. salt
- 1/4 tsp. pepper
- 2 cloves minced garlic
- 3/4 cup whipping cream
- 1 cup broth
- 1 tsp. of poultry seasoning
- 1/4 tsp. of rosemary
- pinch thyme
- 2 1/2 cups diced cooked chicken
- 1/4 tsp. of Xanthan Gum
- For crust:
- 4 1/2 tbsp. melted butter
- 1/3 cup of coconut flour
- 2 tbsp. sour cream
- 4 eggs

- ➢ 1/4 tsp. salt
- ➢ 1/4 tsp. baking powder
- ➢ 1 cup grated cheddar cheese,
- ➢ 1/3 cup grated mozzarella cheese,
- ➢ 1 1/2 tsp. of parsley

Directions:

- ➢ Preheat oven to 400 degrees.
- ➢ Sautee onion, mixed veggies, garlic cloves in butter. Add heavy whipping cream,
- ➢ Chicken broth, and seasoning. Sprinkle Xanthan Gum on top and simmer for 5 minutes. Add diced and cooked chicken.
- ➢ Make the breading by combining melted butter, eggs, salt, sour cream coconut flour, and baking powder. Stir in cheese.
- ➢ Drop batter on chicken pot pie. Bake in a 400-degree oven for 15-20 min.

Nutrition: Calories 376, Fat 11 Fiber: 35 Carbs 1, Protein 28

Slow Cooker Monterey Chicken

Preparation Time: 10 min

Cooking Time: 5 hrs.

Servings: 6

Ingredients

- ➢ 1 sliced onion;1 tbsp. chili powder
- ➢ 1/2 cup of barbeque sauce
- ➢ 1 tbsp. Dijon mustard
- ➢ 2 lb. chicken thighs; salt & pepper
- ➢ 2 diced tomatoes
- ➢ 1 1/2 cups jack cheese shredded
- ➢ 4-6 cups rice cooked
- ➢ 1 avocado cubed
- ➢ 4 slices cooked and chopped bacon

Directions:

- ➢ Brown onion with seasoning into the slow cooker, then add chicken and cook till tender. When cooked, shred it into bite-size pieces and cook again with added tomatoes and stir with sauce. Sprinkle cheese over chicken and cook until melted. Put chicken and sauce over rice, topped with diced avocado and crisp bacon.

Nutrition: Calories 156, Fat 12 Fiber: 3, Carbs 3, Protein 24

Slow Cooker Cauliflower Rice Greek Chicken Bowls

Preparation Time: 40 min

Cooking Time: 5 hrs.

Servings: 8

Ingredients

- ➢ 4 chicken breasts
- ➢ 2 lemons zest & juice
- ➢ 1 tbsp. Greek seasoning
- ➢ 2 tbsp. EVOO
- ➢ 1/2 tsp. oregano
- ➢ 1/2 tsp. black pepper
- ➢ Ingredients for Cauliflower Rice:
- ➢ 20 oz. cauliflower rice, frozen
- ➢ 1 chopped bell pepper
- ➢ 1 small chopped onion
- ➢ 1 tbsp. EVOO
- ➢ 1 tsp. of Greek seasoning
- ➢ salt & black pepper
- ➢ Greek Salsa Ingredients:
- ➢ 3 medium chopped cucumbers,
- ➢ 1 cup cherry tomatoes chopped
- ➢ 1/4 cup Kalamata olives chopped
- ➢ 1/4 cup chopped red onion

> ➢ 4 oz. Feta Cheese crumbled
> ➢ 1/4 cup Italian dressing of your choice

Directions:

> ➢ Cook chicken in Greek Seasoning, lemon, olive oil, Greek oregano, and black pepper together. When tender, shred chicken and coat it in the sauce. Cook cauliflower rice with green pepper, onion, Greek seasoning, salt, and black pepper. Chop the cucumbers, tomatoes, olives, red onion, and mix them with Italian dressing and crumbled feta.

> ➢ To assemble, put cauliflower rice in the bottom of the serving bowl, then place shredded lemon chicken topped with Greek salsa mixture.

Nutrition: Calories 389, Fat 18 Fiber: 6, Carbs 1, Protein 21

Creamy Mexican Slow Cooker Chicken

Preparation Time: 5 min

Cooking Time: 6 hrs.

Servings: 6

Ingredients

- ➢ 1 cup of sour cream
- ➢ 1/2 cup of chicken stock
- ➢ 14 oz. green chilies and tomatoes
- ➢ 1 batch of taco seasoning
- ➢ 2 lb. of chicken breast

Directions:

- ➢ Mix all ingredients in a slow cooker and add chicken. Heat slow cooker on the low setting.
- ➢ To the slow cooker, add the sour cream, chicken stock, diced tomatoes with green chilies, and taco seasoning. Mix until all ingredients are well combined.
- ➢ Add chicken to slow cooker. Cover and cook on low for 6 hours.

Nutrition: Calories 156, Fat 12 Fiber: 3, Carbs 3, Protein 24

Low-Carb Slow Cooker Sour Cream Chicken Enchiladas

Preparation Time: 40 min

Cooking Time: 3 hrs.

Servings: 10

Ingredients

- 1/2 cup Picante sauce
- 30 oz. enchilada sauce
- 6 cups shredded chicken
- 1 cup of sour cream
- 3 cups cheese Mexican blend
- 10 low-carb tortillas; green onions, to garnish

Directions:

- Put 1/2 cup salsa & red enchilada sauce in a small saucepan and cook over low heat. Put shredded chicken and add 1 cup Sauce, 1 cup sour cream, and 11/2 cups grated cheese. Lay the ten tortillas and spread the filling mixture. Grease crockpot and spread 1/4 cup of sauce on the cooker. Roll up each enchilada tightly and place them in a slow cooker. And spread sauce and cheese on it. Cook it on high temperature for two to three hours until enchiladas are gurgling and cheese is melted.

➢ Freshly made served with garnished green onion and extra sour cream.

Nutrition: Calories 265, Fat 15 Fiber: 5 Carbs 1, Protein 21

Paleo Grilled Chicken with Spiced Creamy Sauce

Preparation Time: 30 min

Cooking Time: 4 hrs.

Servings: 4

Ingredients

- Marinade; 3 tbsp. EVOO
- 4 cloves minced garlic
- 2 tbsp. lemon juice
- 1 tbsp. parsley
- 1/4 tsp. of real salt
- pinch pepper flakes
- 4 chicken thighs or breasts ;Dipping Sauce
- 4 tbsp. mayonnaise
- 1 tbsp. lemon juice
- 1/8 tsp. of black pepper
- 1/4 tsp. cumin; salt

Directions:

- Mix marinade components in a flexible bag with chicken. Chill 4 hours or overnight. Grill approx. 15 minutes each side until done. Serve with pita bread.

Nutrition: Calories 321, Fat 11 Fiber: 8, Carbs 3, Protein 24

Low-Carb Chicken Coconut Curry

Preparation Time: 10 min

Cooking Time: 4 hrs.

Servings: 6

Ingredients

- ➢ 1 sliced onion
- ➢ 2 tbsp. of curry paste
- ➢ 2 cups cubed chicken
- ➢ 1/2 cubed pumpkin
- ➢ 1/2 cup of coconut cream
- ➢ 1/2 cup chopped spinach

Directions:

- ➢ Place the first 5 ingredients in the slow cooker dish. Stir and cook on low heat for 6to 10 hours or high for 4 to 6 hours. Mix time to time to let the flavor blend. Ten minutes before serving, add spinach to it and mix. It will sag and cook. You may add spinach at intervals, wait for the first portion to sag, and then add other.
- ➢ Served with rice garnished with cashews or sprinkle of coconut.

Nutrition: Calories 156, Fat 12 Fiber: 3, Carbs 3, Protein 24

Crock Pot Ranch Chicken

Preparation Time: 5 min

Cooking Time: 4 hrs.

Servings: 6

Ingredients

➢ 2 lb. chicken breasts

➢ 3 tbsp. of butter

➢ 4 oz. of cream cheese

➢ 3 tbsp. ranch mix

Directions:

➢ Place chicken in crockpot. Slit the butter and cream cheese into lumps and put-on chicken. Powder the ranch dressing mix over the chicken. Cook chicken in the crockpot on high for 3-4 hours or low 5-7 hours. Scrap chicken before serving.

➢ Serve Ranch chicken over vegetables, noodles, or rice.

Nutrition: Calories 322, Fat 11 Fiber: 4, Carbs 1, Protein 12

Chicken Enchilada Casserole

Preparation Time: 5 min

Cooking Time: 6 hrs.

Servings: 6

Ingredients

➢ 28 oz. tomato sauce

➢ 2 lb. chicken breast;1 juiced lime

➢ 1 sliced onion;2 tsp. cumin

➢ 1 tsp. garlic powder

➢ 1 tsp. chili powder

➢ 1 cup shredded cheddar cheese

➢ 1/3 cup of sour cream

➢ 1/4 cup chopped cilantro

Directions;

➢ Mix tomato sauce, chicken, sliced onion, lime juice, cumin, garlic powder, and chili powder together in a greased slow cooker. Place on low for 8 hours or high for 6 hours. Shred the chicken into bite-size pieces. Top the mixture with the cheese and place the lid back on until the cheese has liquefied, about 5 minutes.

➢ Serve with sour cream and cilantro.

Nutrition: Calories 156, Fat 12 Fiber: 3, Carbs 3, Protein 24

Keto Crockpot Bacon Ranch Chicken

Preparation Time: 10 min

Cooking Time: 4 hrs.

Servings: 8

Ingredients

- 2 lb. chicken breast
- 1 lb. bacon
- 1/2 cup cream cheese whipped
- 1/2 cup of sour cream
- 1 pack ranch dressing dry
- 1/2 cup of ranch dressing
- 4 cups of Colby-jack cheese
- 1 can Rotel tomatoes and chilis
- salt
- pepper

Directions:

- Blend dry ranch packet, cream cheese, and sour cream together in a bowl. Put chicken breasts into greased crockpot. Spread the mixture on top of the chicken breast. Take 6 pieces of bacon, fold it in half, and place it on top of the chicken. Cook on high for 4 hours. Spout out in the can of rote, 3 cups of cheese, and 1/2 cup ranch salad dressing. Blend well while slicing the chicken. Cook on high

36

for another 10 minutes or so until all of the cheese is liquefied into the chicken. cook the remainder of bacon.

➢ Serve chicken on to plate. Dusting with Bacon and more Colby Jack cheese and salt and pepper to taste. Serve with your preferred veggies.

Nutrition: Calories 109, Fat 12 Fiber: 3, Carbs 5, Protein 24

Crockpot Chicken Cacciatore

Preparation Time: 5 min

Cooking Time: 6 hrs.

Servings: 6

Ingredients

- ➤ 2 lb. chicken breast
- ➤ 15.5 oz. pasta sauce
- ➤ 1 onion
- ➤ 7 oz. mushrooms
- ➤ 1 can tomatoes diced
- ➤ 1 pepper
- ➤ 1/2 cup of parmesan cheese

Directions:

- ➤ Sprig crockpot with nonstick spray. Slice onions, green peppers, and mushrooms. Slit chicken breast into bite-sized pieces. Add the chicken and veggies, pour sauce and diced tomatoes and veggies, add parmesan cheese into the crockpot.
- ➤ Turn the crockpot onto high setting and heat for 6 hours.

Nutrition: Calories 176, Fat 16 Fiber: 5, Carbs 1, Protein 28

Crock-Pot Creamy Italian Chicken and Cauliflower

Preparation Time: 5 min

Cooking Time: 4 hrs.

Servings: 5

Ingredients

- ✓ 2 lb. chicken breast
- ✓ 2 pack Italian dressing mix for salad
- ✓ 3 cups chopped cauliflower
- ✓ 8 oz. sliced button mushrooms
- ✓ 12 oz. sliced cream cheese

Directions:

➤ Put the chicken into the pot of the crock-pot and powdered the chicken with one packet of the Italian mix. Top the chicken with the cauliflower, add cream cheese and mushrooms, and spray them with the second pack of Italian mix. Cover the pot and place on low for 6 hours or high for 4 hours. Shred chicken and mix until all the cream cheese are combined.

➤ Sprinkle with the parsley and enjoy.

Nutrition: Calories 231, Fat 10 Fiber: 7, Carbs 1, Protein 21

Pork Chops

Preparation Time: 5 minutes

Cooking Time: 6 hours

Servings: 8

Ingredients:

- ✓ 2 pounds pasture-raised pork chops
- ✓ 1 teaspoon salt
- ✓ 1 tablespoon dried thyme
- ✓ 1 tablespoon dried rosemary
- ✓ 1 tablespoon ground cumin
- ✓ 1 tablespoon dried curry powder
- ✓ 1 tablespoon chopped fresh chives
- ✓ 1 tablespoon fennel seeds
- ✓ 4 tablespoons avocado oil

Directions:

- ➤ Place 2 tablespoons oil in a small bowl, add remaining ingredients except for pork and stir until well mixed.
- ➤ Rub this mixture on all sides of pork chips until evenly coated.
- ➤ Grease a 6-quart slow cooker with remaining oil, add seasoned pork chops and shut with lid.

➢ Plug in the slow cooker and cook pork for 6 hours at low heat setting or 4 hours at high heat setting.

Nutrition: Calories: 235 Total Fat: 15g Saturated Fat: 3g Protein: 24g Carbs: 1g Fiber: 0g Sugar: 0g

Spicy Pork & Spinach Stew

Preparation Time: 5 minutes

Cooking Time: 4 hours and 20 minutes

Servings: 5

Ingredients:

- ✓ 1 pound pasture-raised pork butt, fat trimmed and cut into 2-inch pieces
- ✓ 6 cups chopped baby spinach
- ✓ 10 ounces Rote tomatoes
- ✓ 1 large white onion, peeled and quartered
- ✓ 4 cloves of garlic, peeled
- ✓ 1 teaspoon dried thyme
- ✓ 2 teaspoons Cajun seasoning blend
- ✓ 4 tablespoons avocado oil
- ✓ 3/4 cup heavy whipping cream

Directions:

- ➤ Place tomatoes, onion and garlic in a food processor and pulse for 1 to 2 minutes or until blended.
- ➤ Pour this mixture in a 6-quart slow cooker, add Cajun seasoning mix, thyme, avocado oil, and pork pieces and stir well until evenly coated.

- ➢ Plug in the slow cooker, then shut with lid and cook for 5 hours at low heat setting or 2 hours at high heat setting.
- ➢ When done, stir in cream until combined, add spinach and continue cooking at low heat setting for 20 minutes or more until spinach wilts.
- ➢ Serve straightaway.

Nutrition: Calories: 604 Total Fat: 38.3g Saturated Fat: 9g Protein: 56g Carbs: 9g Fiber: 5g; Sugar: 4g

Stuffed Taco Peppers

Preparation Time: 5 minutes

Cooking Time: 8 hours

Servings: 6

Ingredients:

- ✓ 1 cup cauliflower rice
- ✓ 6 small red bell peppers
- ✓ 18-ounce minced pork, pasture-raised
- ✓ 1 teaspoon garlic powder
- ✓ 3/4 teaspoon salt
- ✓ 1 teaspoon red chili powder
- ✓ 1 cup shredded Monterey jack cheese and more for topping
- ✓ 2 tablespoons avocado oil
- ✓ 1 cup water

Directions:

- ➢ Remove and discard stem from each pepper and then scoop out seeds.
- ➢ Place meat in a large bowl, add garlic, salt, and red chili powder and stir until combined.
- ➢ Then stir in cauliflower rice and oil until just combine and then stir in cheese.
- ➢ Stuff this mixture into each pepper and place them in a 4-quart slow cooker.

➤ Pour water into the bottom of slow cooker, switch it on and shut with the lid.

➤ Cook peppers for 4 hours at high heat setting or 8 hours at low heating setting and top peppers with more cheese in the last 10 minutes of cooking time.

➤ Serve straightaway.

Nutrition: Calories: 270 Total Fat: 18g Saturated Fat: 5g Protein: 21g Carbs: 6g Fiber: 2g Sugar: 3g

Chinese Pulled Pork

Preparation Time: 5 minutes

Cooking Time: 7 hours and 30 minutes

Servings: 6

Ingredients:

- ✓ 2.2-pound pasture-raised pork shoulder, fat trimmed
- ✓ 2 tablespoons garlic paste
- ✓ 2 teaspoons ginger paste
- ✓ 1 teaspoon smoked paprika
- ✓ 5 drops Erythritol sweetener
- ✓ 4 tablespoons soy sauce
- ✓ 1 tablespoon tomato paste
- ✓ 4 tablespoons tomato sauce, sugar-free
- ✓ 1 cup chicken broth

Directions:

- ➢ Place pork in a 6-quart slow cooker.
- ➢ Whisk together remaining ingredients until smooth and then pour over the pork.
- ➢ Plug in the slow cooker, then shut with lid and cook for 7 hours at low heat setting or until pork is tender.
- ➢ Then shred pork with two forks and stir well until evenly coated with sauce.

- ➢ Continue cooking pork for 30 minutes or more at low heating setting until sauce is thicken to desired consistency.
- ➢ Serve straightaway.

Nutrition: Calories: 447 Total Fat: 35g Saturated Fat: 13g Protein: 30g Carbs: 3g Fiber: 1g Sugar: 2g

Bacon Wrapped Pork Loin

Preparation Time: 5 minutes

Cooking Time: 7 hours

Servings: 4

Ingredients:

- ✓ 2-pound pasture-raised pork loin roast, fat-trimmed
- ✓ 4 strips of bacon, uncooked
- ✓ 3 tablespoon dried onion soup mix, organic
- ✓ 1/4 cup water

Directions:

- ➢ Pour water into a 6-quart slow cooker.
- ➢ Rub seasoning mix on all sides of pork, then wrap with bacon and place into the slow cooker.
- ➢ Plug in the slow cooker, then shut with lid and cook for 7 hours at low heat setting or 5 hours at high heat setting.
- ➢ Serve straightaway.

Nutrition: Calories: 639 Total Fat: 41g Saturated Fat: 19g Protein: 69g Carbs: 0g Fiber: 0g Sugar: 0g

Lamb Barbacoa

Preparation Time: 5 minutes

Cooking Time: 8 hours

Servings: 12

Ingredients:

- ✓ 5 pounds pasture-raised pork shoulder,
- ✓ 2 tablespoons salt
- ✓ 1 teaspoon chipotle powder
- ✓ 2 tablespoons smoked paprika
- ✓ 1 tablespoon ground cumin
- ✓ 1 tablespoon dried oregano
- ✓ 1/4 cup dried mustard ;1 cup water

Directions:

- ➢ Stir together salt, chipotle powder, paprika, cumin, oregano, and mustard and rub this mixture generously on all over the pork.
- ➢ Place seasoned pork into a 6-quart slow cooker, plug it in, then shut with lid and cook for 6 hours at high heat setting.
- ➢ When done, shred pork with two forks and stir well until coated well. Serve straightaway.

Nutrition: Calories: 477 Total Fat: 35.8g Saturated Fat: 14.8g Protein: 37.5g Carbs: 1.2g Fiber: 0.5g Sugar: 5g

Balsamic Pork Tenderloin

Preparation Time: 5 minutes

Cooking Time: 6 hours

Servings: 8

Ingredients:

- ✓ 2 pounds pasture-raised pork tenderloin
- ✓ 2 teaspoons minced garlic
- ✓ 1/2 teaspoon sea salt
- ✓ 1/2 teaspoon red pepper flakes
- ✓ 1 tablespoon Worcestershire sauce
- ✓ 2 tablespoons avocado oil
- ✓ 1/2 cup balsamic vinegar
- ✓ 2 tablespoons coconut aminos

Directions:

- ➤ Grease a 6-quart slow cooker with oil and set aside.
- ➤ Sprinkle garlic all over the pork and then place it into the slow cooker.
- ➤ Whisk together remaining ingredients, then pour over pork and shut with lid.
- ➤ Plug in the slow cooker and cook pork for 6 hours at low heat setting or 4 hours at high setting until tender.

➤ When done, transfer pork to serving plate, pour 1/2 cup of cooking liquid over pork and serve.

Nutrition: Calories: 224 Total Fat: 10g Saturated Fat: 1.6g Protein: 33g Carbs: 0.6g Fiber: 0g Sugar: 0.3g

Spicy Pork

Preparation Time: 5 minutes

Cooking Time: 10 hours

Servings: 6

Ingredients:

- ✓ 2 pasture-raised pork shoulder, boneless and fat trimmed
- ✓ 1/2 of jalapeno, deseeded and cored, chopped
- ✓ 6-ounce crushed tomatoes
- ✓ 1/4 cup chopped green onion
- ✓ 3 cloves of garlic, peeled and sliced in half
- ✓ 1 tablespoon sea salt
- ✓ 1/2 teaspoon ground black pepper
- ✓ 1 1/2 tablespoon paprika, divided
- ✓ 1/2 tablespoon dried oregano
- ✓ 1/2 tablespoon ground cumin
- ✓ 2 limes, juiced
- ✓ 2 tablespoons avocado oil

Directions:

- ➤ Place pork in a 6-quart slow cooker, season with salt, black pepper, paprika, oregano, and cumin until seasoned well.
- ➤ Then add remaining ingredients and stir until combined.

➤ Plug in the slow cooker, shut it with the lid and cook for 8 to 10 hours at low heat setting or 4 to 5 hours at high heat setting until very tender.

➤ Serve straightaway.

Nutrition: Calories: 344.5 Total Fat: 25g Saturated Fat: 10.7g Protein: 28.4g Carbs: 1.7g Fiber: 0.5g Sugar: 1.1g

Zesty Garlic Pulled Pork

Preparation Time: 5 minutes

Cooking Time: 8 hours

Servings: 6

Ingredients:

✓ 3-pound pasture-raised pork shoulder

✓ 5 cloves of garlic, peeled and sliced

✓ 1 tablespoon of salt

✓ 1/2 teaspoon ground black pepper

✓ 1 teaspoon oregano

✓ 1/2 teaspoon cumin

✓ 1 lime, zested and juiced

Directions:

➢ Make cut into the meat of pork and stuff with garlic slices.

➢ Stir together garlic, salt, black pepper, oregano, cumin, lime zest, and juice until smooth paste comes together and then brush this paste all over the pork.

➢ Place pork into a large resealable bag, seal it and let marinate in the refrigerator for overnight.

➢ When ready to cook, transfer pork to a 6-quart slow cooker and shut with lid.

➢ Plug in the slow cooker and cook for 8 hours at low heat setting or until pork is very tender.

➢ When done, shred pork with two forks and serve as a lettuce wrap.

Nutrition: Calories: 616 Total Fat: 43g Saturated Fat: 11.5g Protein: 55.4g Carbs: 1.5g Fiber: 0.3g Sugar: 0g

Ranch Pork Chops

Preparation Time: 5 minutes

Cooking Time: 8 hours

Servings: 6

Ingredients:

- ✓ 8-ounce sliced mushrooms
- ✓ 2 pounds pasture-raised pork loin
- ✓ 2 tablespoons ranch dressing mix
- ✓ 2 tablespoons avocado oil
- ✓ 21-ounce cream of chicken soup
- ✓ 2 cups water

Directions:

- ➢ Add ranch dressing, oil chicken soup, and water into the bowl, whisk until smooth, then add mushrooms and stir until combined.
- ➢ Cut pork into 6 slices and layer into the bottom of a slow cooker.
- ➢ Evenly pour in prepared chicken soup mixture and shut with lid.
- ➢ Plug in the slow cooker and cook for 8 hours at low heat setting or until pork is cooked through.

Nutrition: Calories: 479 Total Fat: 27g Saturated Fat: 12g Protein: 54g Carbs: 5g Fiber: 1g Sugar: 1.5g

Pork Chile Verde

Preparation Time: 5 minutes

Cooking Time: 7 hours and 5 minutes

Servings: 6

Ingredients:

✓ 2 pounds pasture-raised pork shoulder, cut into 6 pieces

✓ 1 teaspoon sea salt

✓ 1/2 teaspoon ground black pepper

✓ 1 1/2 tablespoon avocado oil

✓ 1 1/2 cup salsa Verde

✓ 1 cup chicken broth

Directions:

➤ Season pork with salt and black pepper.

➤ Place a large skillet pan over medium heat, add oil and when hot, add seasoned pork pieces.

➤ Cook pork for 3 to 4 minutes per side or until browned and then transfer to a 6-quart slow cooker.

➤ Whisk together salsa and chicken broth and pour over pork pieces.

➤ Plug in the slow cooker, then shut with lid and cook for 6 to 7 hours at low heat setting or until pork is very tender.

➢ When done, shred pork with two forks and stir until combined.

Nutrition: Calories: 342 Total Fat: 22g Saturated Fat: 12g Protein: 32g Carbs: 5 g Fiber: 2g Sugar: 4g

Ham Soup

Preparation Time: 5 minutes

Cooking Time: 4 hours

Servings: 6

Ingredients:

- ✓ 2 pounds pasture-raised smoked ham hock
- ✓ 4 cups cauliflower florets; 2 bay leaves
- ✓ 1/4 teaspoon nutmeg
- ✓ 3 cups bone broth

Directions:

- ➢ Place cauliflower florets in a 6-quarts slow cooker, add remaining ingredients and pour in water until all the ingredients are just submerged.
- ➢ Plug in the slow cooker, then shut with lid and cook for 4 hours at high heat setting or until cauliflower florets are very tender.
- ➢ Transfer ham to a bowl, shred with two forms and discard bone and fat pieces.
- ➢ Puree cauliflower in the slow cooker with a stick blender for 1 to 2 minutes or until smooth, return shredded ham and stir until well combined.

Nutrition: Calories: 349 Total Fat: 23g Saturated Fat: 10g Protein: 34g Carbs: 5g Fiber: 2g Sugar: 2g

Beef and Broccoli

Preparation Time: 5 minutes

Cooking Time: 25 minutes

Servings: 4

Ingredients:

- ✓ 1 1/2-pound Chuck roast, sliced
- ✓ 12 ounces Broccoli florets
- ✓ 4 Garlic cloves, peeled
- ✓ 2 tablespoons Avocado oil
- ✓ 1/2 cup Soy sauce
- ✓ 1/4 cup Erythritol sweetener
- ✓ 1 tablespoon Xanthan gum

Directions:

➢ Switch on the instant pot, grease pot with oil, press the 'sauté/simmer' button, wait until the oil is hot and add the beef slices and garlic and cook for 5 to 10 minutes or until browned.

➢ Meanwhile, whisk together sweetener, soy sauce, and broth until combined.

➢ Pour sauce over browned beef, toss until well coated, then press the 'keep warm' button and shut the instant pot with its lid in the sealed position.

➢ Press the 'manual' button, press '+/-' to set the cooking time to 10 minutes and cook at high-pressure setting; when the pressure builds in the pot, the cooking timer will start.

➢ Meanwhile, place broccoli florets in a large heatproof bowl, cover with plastic wrap and microwave for 4 minutes or until tender.

➢ When the instant pot buzzes, press the 'keep warm' button, do a quick pressure release and open the lid.

➢ Take out 1/4 cup of cooking liquid, stir in xanthan gum until combined, then add into the instant pot and stir until mixed.

➢ Press the 'sauté/simmer' button and simmer beef and sauce for 5 minutes or until the sauce reaches desired consistency.

➢ Then add broccoli florets, stir until mixed and press the cancel button.

➢ **Serve broccoli and beef with cauliflower rice.**

Nutrition: Calories: 351.4 Fat: 12.4 g Protein: 29 g Carbs: 1.1 g Fiber: 8 g

Korean Barbecue Beef

Preparation Time: 5 minutes

Cooking Time: 25 minutes

Servings: 4

Ingredients:

- ✓ 3 pounds Beef chuck roast, fat trimmed, cubed
- ✓ 1/2 cup Beef broth
- ✓ 1/3 cup Erythritol sweetener –
- ✓ 1/4 cup Liquid aminos –
- ✓ 2 tablespoons Minced garlic
- ✓ 2 tablespoons Avocado oil
- ✓ 1 tablespoon Apple cider vinegar –
- ✓ 1 tablespoon Grated ginger
- ✓ 1 1/2 teaspoon Sriracha sauce –
- ✓ 1/2 teaspoon Ground black pepper

Directions:

- ➢ Switch on the instant pot, add all the ingredients, and stir until mixed.
- ➢ Shut the instant pot with its lid in the sealed position, then press the 'manual' button, press '+/-' to set the cooking time to 25 minutes and cook at high-pressure setting; when the pressure builds in the pot, the cooking timer will start.

➢ When the instant pot buzzes, press the 'keep warm' button, release pressure naturally for 10 minutes, then do a quick pressure release and open the lid.

➢ Garnish beef with cilantro and serve.

Nutrition: Calories: 635.7 Fat: 31.7 g Protein: 69.3 g Carbs: 5 g Fiber: 17.3 g

Whole Chicken

Preparation Time: 5 minutes

Cooking Time: 25 minutes

Servings: 7

Ingredients:

- ✓ 5 pounds Medium whole chicken –
- ✓ 1 1/2 teaspoon Minced garlic
- ✓ 1 tablespoon Avocado oil
- ✓ 1/8 teaspoon Sea salt
- ✓ 1/4 teaspoon Ground black pepper
- ✓ 1 Lemon, sliced
- ✓ 2 cups Water –
- ✓ 1 tablespoon Apple cider vinegar

Directions:

- ➢ Brush chicken with oil, then rub with salt and black pepper and stuff its cavity with lemon slices.
- ➢ Switch on the instant pot, pour in water, add vinegar, then place the chicken on it and shut the instant pot with its lid in the sealed position.
- ➢ Press the 'manual' button, press '+/-' to set the cooking time to 25 minutes and cook at high-pressure setting; when the pressure builds in the pot, the cooking timer will start.

- ➤ When the instant pot buzzes, press the 'keep warm' button, release pressure naturally for 10 minutes, then do a quick pressure release and open the lid.
- ➤ Transfer chicken to a cutting board, let it rest for 10 minutes, then cut into pieces and serve.

Nutrition: Calories: 209 Fat: 5 g Protein: 41 g Carbs: 1 g Fiber: 0 g

Garlic Chicken

Preparation Time: 5 minutes

Cooking Time: 35 minutes

Servings: 4

Ingredients:

- ✓ 4 Chicken breasts
- ✓ 1 teaspoon Salt
- ✓ 1/4 cup Avocado oil
- ✓ 1 teaspoon Turmeric powder
- ✓ 10 Cloves of garlic, peeled and diced

Directions:

- ➢ Switch on the instant pot, add chicken, then season with salt and black pepper, pour in the oil and scatter garlic on top.
- ➢ Shut the instant pot with its lid in the sealed position, then press the 'manual' button, press '+/-' to set the cooking time to 35 minutes and cook at high-pressure setting; when the pressure builds in the pot, the cooking timer will start.
- ➢ When the instant pot buzzes, press the 'keep warm' button, release pressure naturally for 10 minutes, then do a quick pressure release and open the lid.

➢ Shred chicken with two forks, toss until mixed and serve as a lettuce wrap.

Nutrition: Calories: 404 Fat: 21 g Protein: 47 g Carbs: 3 g Fiber: 0 g

Lamb Shanks

Preparation Time: 5 minutes

Cooking Time: 1 hour and 30 minutes

Servings: 2

Ingredients:

- ✓ 1/4 cup Avocado oil
- ✓ 2.5 pounds Lamb shanks
- ✓ 1 tablespoon Minced garlic
- ✓ 1 Medium white onion, peeled and diced
- ✓ 2 Sticks of celery, diced
- ✓ 2 tablespoons Rosemary
- ✓ 1 teaspoon Salt
- ✓ 1/2 teaspoon Ground black pepper
- ✓ 1 cup Lamb or chicken broth
- ✓ 14 ounces Diced tomatoes

Directions:

➢ Switch on the instant pot, add half of the oil, press the 'sauté/simmer' button, wait until the oil is hot and lamb shanks in a single layer and cook for 3 to 5 minutes per side or until browned.

➢ Transfer lamb shanks to a plate, set aside, then add onion, celery, garlic, and rosemary into the instant pot and cook for 3 minutes.

➢ Season with salt and black pepper, pour in the broth, mix well, then add tomatoes, return lamb shanks into the pot and toss until combined.

➢ Press the 'keep warm' button, shut the instant pot with its lid in the sealed position, then press the 'manual' button, press '+/-' to set the cooking time to 50 minutes and cook at high-pressure setting; when the pressure builds in the pot, the cooking timer will start.

➢ When the instant pot buzzes, press the 'keep warm' button, release pressure naturally for 10 minutes, then do a quick pressure release and open the lid.

➢ Transfer lamb shanks to a dish, then press the 'sauté/simmer' button and simmer the sauce for 5 minutes or more until the sauce is reduced by half.

➢ Ladle sauce over the lamb shanks and serve.

Nutrition: Calories: 410 Fat: 35 g Protein: 51 g Carbs: 1.2 g Fiber: 3 g

Jamaican Jerk Pork Roast

Preparation Time: 5 minutes

Cooking Time: 1 hour and 5 minutes

Servings: 4

Ingredients:

- ✓ 4 pounds Pork shoulder, fat trimmed
- ✓ 1/4 cup Jamaican jerk spice mix
- ✓ 2 tablespoons Avocado oil
- ✓ 1/2 cup Beef broth

Directions:

- ➢ Brush pork shoulder with 1 tablespoon oil and then sprinkle with spice mix until evenly coated on all sides.
- ➢ Switch on the instant pot, grease pot with oil, press the 'sauté/simmer' button, wait until the oil is hot, add pork shoulder and cook for 5 minutes per side or until nicely browned.
- ➢ Pour in beef broth,
- ➢ Press the 'keep warm' button, shut the instant pot with its lid in the sealed position, then press the 'manual' button, press '+/-' to set the cooking time to 45 minutes and cook at high-pressure setting; when the pressure builds in the pot, the cooking timer will start.

➢ When the instant pot buzzes, press the 'keep warm' button, release pressure naturally for 10 minutes, then do a quick pressure release and open the lid.

➢ Shred the pork with two forks, toss until mixed and serve.

Nutrition: Calories: 282 Fat: 20 g Protein: 23 g Carbs: 0 g Fiber: 0 g

Salmon

Preparation Time: 5 minutes

Cooking Time: 5 minutes

Servings: 4

Ingredients:

- ✓ 3 lemon, sliced
- ✓ 3/4 cup Water
- ✓ 4 Salmon fillets
- ✓ 1 Bunch of dill weed, fresh
- ✓ 1 tablespoon Butter, unsalted
- ✓ 1/4 teaspoon Salt
- ✓ 1/4 teaspoon Ground black pepper

Directions:

➢ Switch on the instant pot, pour in water, stir in lemon juice, and insert a steel steamer rack.

➢ Place salmon on the steamer rack, sprinkle with dill and then top with lemon slices.

➢ Press the 'keep warm' button, shut the instant pot with its lid in the sealed position, then press the 'manual' button, press '+/-' to set the cooking time to 5 minutes and cook at high-pressure setting; when the pressure builds in the pot, the cooking timer will start.

➢ When the instant pot buzzes, press the 'keep warm' button, do a quick pressure release and open the lid.

➢ Remove and discard the lemon slices, transfer salmon to a dish, season with salt and black pepper, garnish with more dill and serve with lemon wedges and cauliflower rice.

Nutrition: Calories: 199.2; Fat: 8.1 g Protein: 29.2 g Carbs: 0.8 g Fiber: 0.1 g

Coconut Chicken

Preparation Time: 5 minutes

Cooking Time: 22 minutes

Servings: 4

Ingredients:

- ✓ 1 Bunch of celery, chopped
- ✓ 1 pound Chicken breast, cubed
- ✓ 1 cup Chicken broth
- ✓ 5 Stalks of lemongrass
- ✓ 1 cup Coconut milk
- ✓ 3/4 teaspoon   Salt
- ✓ 1/2 teaspoon Ground black pepper

Directions:

➤ Switch on the instant pot, add celery, then top with chicken, add lemongrass and pour in chicken broth.

➤ Shut the instant pot with its lid in the sealed position, then press the 'manual' button, press '+/-' to set the cooking time to 22 minutes and cook at high-pressure setting; when the pressure builds in the pot, the cooking timer will start.

➤ When the instant pot buzzes, press the 'keep warm' button, do a quick pressure release and open the lid.

➤ Remove and discard lemongrass, season with salt and black pepper, then pour in coconut milk and stir until combined.

➤ Serve coconut chicken with cauliflower rice.

Nutrition: Calories: 260 Fat: 15.1 g Protein: 27.8 g Carbs: 1 g Fiber: 2.2 g

Mahi Taco Wraps

Preparation Time: 5 minutes

Cooking Time: 2 hours

Servings: 6

Ingredients:

- ✓ 1pound Mahi Mahi, wild-caught
- ✓ 1/2 cup cherry tomatoes
- ✓ 1 small green bell pepper, cored and sliced
- ✓ 1/4 of a medium red onion, thinly sliced
- ✓ 1/2 teaspoon garlic powder
- ✓ 1 teaspoon sea salt
- ✓ 1/2 teaspoon ground black pepper
- ✓ 1 teaspoon chipotle pepper
- ✓ 1/2 teaspoon dried oregano
- ✓ 1 teaspoon cumin
- ✓ 1tablespoons avocado oil
- ✓ 1/4 cup chicken stock
- ✓ 1 medium avocado, diced
- ✓ 1 cup sour cream
- ✓ 6 large lettuce leaves

Directions:

- ➢ Grease a 6-quarts slow cooker with oil, place fish in it and then pour in chicken stock.

➢ Stir together garlic powder, salt, black pepper, chipotle pepper, oregano and cumin and then season fish with half of this mixture.

➢ Layer fish with tomatoes, pepper and onion, season with remaining spice mixture and shut with lid.

➢ Plug in the slow cooker and cook fish for 2 hours at high heat setting or until cooked through.

➢ When done, evenly spoon fish among lettuce, top with avocado and sour cream and serve.

Nutrition: Calories: 260 Fat: 15.1 g Protein: 27.8 g Carbs: 1.9 g Fiber: 2.2 g Sugar: 3

Shrimp Tacos

Preparation Time: 5 minutes

Cooking Time: 3 hours

Servings: 6

Ingredients:

- ✓ 1pound medium wild-caught shrimp, peeled and tails off
- ✓ 12-ounce fire-roasted tomatoes, diced
- ✓ 1small green bell pepper, chopped
- ✓ 1/2cup chopped white onion
- ✓ 1teaspoon minced garlic
- ✓ 1/2teaspoon sea salt
- ✓ 1/2teaspoon ground black pepper
- ✓ 1/2teaspoon red chili powder
- ✓ 1/2teaspoon cumin
- ✓ 1/4 teaspoon cayenne pepper
- ✓ 2tablespoons avocado oil
- ✓ 1/2cup salsa
- ✓ 4tablespoons chopped cilantro
- ✓ 11/2cup sour cream
- ✓ 2medium avocado, diced

Directions:

- ➤ Rinse shrimps, layer into a 6-quarts slow cooker and drizzle with oil.

➤ Add tomatoes, stir until mixed, then add peppers and remaining ingredients except for sour cream and avocado and stir until combined.

➤ Plug in the slow cooker, shut with lid and cook for 2 to 3 hours at low heat setting or 1 hour and 30 minutes to 2 hours at high heat setting or until shrimps turn pink.

➤ When done, serve shrimps with avocado and sour cream.

Nutrition: Calories: 324 Fat: 12 g Protein: 28 g Carbs: 4.2 g Fiber: 13 gSugar: 2g

Fish Curry

Preparation Time: 5 minutes

Cooking Time: 4 hours

Servings: 6

Ingredients:

- ✓ 2.2pounds wild-caught white fish fillet, cubed
- ✓ 18-ounce spinach leaves
- ✓ 4tablespoons red curry paste, organic
- ✓ 14-ounce coconut cream, unsweetened and full-fat;14-ounce water

Directions:

- ➤ Plug in a 6-quart slow cooker and let preheat at high heat setting.
- ➤ In the meantime, whisk together coconut cream and water until smooth.
- ➤ Place fish into the slow cooker, spread with curry paste and then pour in coconut cream mixture.
- ➤ Shut with lid and cook for 2 hours at high heat setting or 4 hours at low heat setting until tender.
- ➤ Then add spinach and continue cooking for 20 to 30 minutes or until spinach leaves wilt.
- ➤ **Nutrition: Calories: 129 Fat: 6 g Protein: 12 g Carbs: 4.8 g Fiber: 10 g Sugar: 6g**

Salmon with Creamy Lemon Sauce

Preparation Time: 5 minutes

Cooking Time: 2 hours

Servings: 6

Ingredients:

- ✓ For the Salmon:
- ✓ 2pounds wild-caught salmon fillet, skin-on
- ✓ 1teaspoon garlic powder
- ✓ 11/2 teaspoon salt
- ✓ 1teaspoon ground black pepper
- ✓ 1/2teaspoon red chili powder
- ✓ 1teaspoon Italian Seasoning
- ✓ 1lemon, sliced
- ✓ 1lemon, juiced
- ✓ 2tablespoons avocado oil
- ✓ 1cup chicken broth
- ✓ For the Creamy Lemon Sauce:
- ✓ Chopped parsley, for garnish
- ✓ 1/8teaspoon lemon zest
- ✓ 1/4cup heavy cream
- ✓ 1/4cup grated parmesan cheese

Direction:

- ➤ Line a 6-quart slow cooker with parchment sheet, spread its bottom with lemon slices, then top with salmon and drizzle with oil.
- ➤ Stir together garlic powder, salt, black pepper, red chili powder, Italian seasoning, and oil until combined and rub this mixture all over salmon.
- ➤ Pour lemon juice and broth around the fish and shut with lid.
- ➤ Plug in the slow cooker and cook for 2 hours at low heat setting.
- ➤ In the meantime, set the oven at 400 degrees F and let preheat.
- ➤ When fish is done, lift out an inner pot of slow cooker, place into the oven and cook for 5 to 8 minutes or until top is nicely browned.
- ➤ Lift out fish using parchment sheet and keep it warm.
- ➤ Transfer juices from slow cooker to a medium skillet pan, place it over medium-high heat, then bring to boil and cook for 1 minute.
- ➤ Turn heat to a low level, whisk cream into the sauce along with lemon zest and parmesan

cheese and cook for 2 to 3 minutes or until thickened.

➤ Cut salmon in pieces, then top each piece with lemon sauce and serve.

Nutrition: Calories: 364 Fat: 19 g Protein: 12.9 g Carbs: 3.8 g Fiber: 7 g Sugar: 9 g

Salmon with Lemon-Caper Sauce

Preparation Time: 5 minutes

Cooking Time: 1 hour

Servings: 4

Ingredients:

- ✓ 1pound wild-caught salmon fillet
- ✓ 2teaspoon capers, rinsed and mashed
- ✓ 1teaspoon minced garlic
- ✓ 1teaspoon salt
- ✓ 1/2teaspoon ground black pepper
- ✓ 1/2teaspoon dried oregano
- ✓ 1teaspoon lemon zest
- ✓ 2tablespoons lemon juice
- ✓ 4tablespoons unsalted butter

Directions:

- ➢ Cut salmon into 4 pieces, then season with salt and black pepper and sprinkle lemon zest on top.
- ➢ Line a 6-quart slow cooker with parchment paper, place seasoned salmon pieces on it and shut with lid.
- ➢ Plug in the slow cooker and cook for 1 hour and 30 minutes or until salmon is cooked through.
- ➢ When 10 minutes of cooking time is left, prepare lemon-caper sauce and for this, place a small

saucepan over low heat, add butter and let it melt.

➢ Then add capers, garlic, lemon juice, stir until mixed and simmer for 1 minute.

➢ Remove saucepan from heat and stir in oregano.

➢ When salmon is cooked, spoon lemon-caper sauce on it and serve.

Nutrition: Calories: 421 Fat: 11 g Protein: 13.8 g Carbs: 2.4 g Fiber: 7 g Sugar: 8 g

Spicy Barbecue Shrimp

Preparation Time: 5 minutes

Cooking Time: 1 hour

Servings: 6

Ingredients:

- ✓ 11/2pounds large wild-caught shrimp, unpeeled
- ✓ 1green onion, chopped;1teaspoon minced garlic
- ✓ 11/2teaspoon salt
- ✓ 3/4teaspoon ground black pepper
- ✓ 1teaspoon Cajun seasoning
- ✓ 1tablespoon hot pepper sauce
- ✓ 1/4cup Worcestershire Sauce
- ✓ 1lemon, juiced
- ✓ 2tablespoons avocado oil
- ✓ 1/2cup unsalted butter, chopped

Directions:

- ➤ Place all the ingredients except for shrimps in a 6-quart slow cooker and whisk until mixed.
- ➤ Plug in the slow cooker, then shut with lid and cook for 30 minutes at high heat setting.
- ➤ Then take out 1/2 cup of this sauce and reserve.
- ➤ Add shrimps to slow cooker.

Nutrition: Calories: 313 Fat: 15 g Protein: 13.8 g Carbs: 2.6 g Fiber: 7 g Sugar: 7 g

Lemon Dill Halibut

Preparation Time: 5 minutes

Cooking Time: 2 hours

Servings: 6

Ingredients:

- ✓ 12-ounce wild-caught halibut fillet
- ✓ 1teaspoon salt ;1/2teaspoon ground black pepper
- ✓ 11/2 teaspoon dried dill
- ✓ 1tablespoon fresh lemon juice
- ✓ 3tablespoons avocado oil

Directions:

- ➤ Cut an 18-inch piece of aluminum foil, place halibut fillet in the middle and then season with salt and black pepper.
- ➤ Whisk together remaining ingredients, drizzle this mixture over halibut, then crimp the edges of foil and place it into a 6-quart slow cooker.
- ➤ Plug in the slow cooker, shut with lid and cook for 1 hour and 30 minutes or 2 hours at high heat setting or until cooked through.
- ➤ When done, carefully open the crimped edges and check the fish, it should be tender and flaky.

Nutrition: Calories: 312 Fat: 15 g Protein: 13.8 g Carbs: 0 g Fiber: 7 g Sugar: 0 g

Coconut Cilantro Curry Shrimp

Preparation Time: 5 minutes

Cooking Time: 2 hours

Servings: 4

Ingredients:

- ✓ 1pound wild-caught shrimp, peeled and deveined
- ✓ 21/2teaspoon lemon garlic seasoning
- ✓ 2tablespoons red curry paste
- ✓ 4tablespoons chopped cilantro
- ✓ 30ounces coconut milk, unsweetened
- ✓ 16ounces water

Directions:

- ➢ Whisk together all the ingredients except for shrimps and 2 tablespoons cilantro and add to a 4-quart slow cooker.
- ➢ Plug in the slow cooker, shut with lid and cook for 2 hours at high heat setting or 4 hours at low heat setting.
- ➢ Then add shrimps, toss until evenly coated and cook for 20 to 30 minutes at high heat settings or until shrimps are pink.
- ➢ Garnish shrimps with remaining cilantro and serve

Nutrition: Calories: 213 Fat: 12 g Protein: 15 g Carbs: 1.9 g Fiber: 7 g Sugar: 1.4 g

Shrimp in Marinara Sauce

Preparation Time: 5 minutes

Cooking Time: 5 hours

Servings: 5

Ingredients:

- ✓ 1pound cooked wild-caught shrimps, peeled and deveined
- ✓ 14.5ounce crushed tomatoes
- ✓ 1/2teaspoon minced garlic
- ✓ 1teaspoon salt
- ✓ 1/2teaspoon seasoned salt
- ✓ 1/4teaspoon ground black pepper
- ✓ 1/2teaspoon crushed red pepper flakes
- ✓ 1/2teaspoon dried basil
- ✓ 1/2teaspoon dried oregano
- ✓ 1/2tablespoons avocado oil
- ✓ 6-ounce chicken broth
- ✓ 2tablespoon minced parsley
- ✓ 1/2cup grated Parmesan cheese

Directions:

- ➢ Place all the ingredients except for shrimps, parsley, and cheese in a 4-quart slow cooker and stir well.

- ➢ Then plug in the slow cooker, shut with lid and cook for 4 to 5 hours at low heat setting.
- ➢ Then add shrimps and parsley, stir until mixed and cook for 10 minutes at high heat setting.
- ➢ Garnish shrimps with cheese and serve.

Nutrition: Calories: 213 Fat: 12 g Protein: 15 g Carbs: 3.9 g Fiber: 7 g Sugar: 3.6 g

Garlic Shrimp

Preparation Time: 5 minutes

Cooking Time: 5 hours

Servings: 5

Ingredients:

- ✓ For the Garlic Shrimp:
- ✓ 11/2 pounds large wild-caught shrimp, peeled and deveined
- ✓ 1/4teaspoon ground black pepper
- ✓ 1/8teaspoon ground cayenne pepper
- ✓ 2 1/2teaspoons minced garlic
- ✓ 1/4cup avocado oil
- ✓ 4tablespoons unsalted butter
- ✓ For the Seasoning:
- ✓ 1teaspoon onion powder
- ✓ 1tablespoon garlic powder
- ✓ 1tablespoon salt
- ✓ 2teaspoons ground black pepper
- ✓ 1tablespoon paprika
- ✓ 1teaspoon cayenne pepper
- ✓ 1teaspoon dried oregano
- ✓ 1teaspoon dried thyme

Directions:

➤ Stir together all the ingredients for seasoning, garlic, oil, and butter and add to a 4-quart slow cooker.

➤ Plug in the slow cooker, shut with lid and cook for 25 to 30 minutes at high heat setting or until cooked.

➤ Then add shrimps, toss until evenly coated and continue cooking for 20 to 30 minutes at high heat setting or until shrimps are pink.

➤ When done, transfer shrimps to a serving plate, top with sauce and serve.

Nutrition: Calories: 227 Fat: 13 g Protein: 21 g Carbs: 1.2 g Fiber: 7 g Sugar: 5 g

Poached Salmon

Preparation Time: 5 minutes

Cooking Time: 3 hours

Servings: 4

Ingredients:

- ✓ 4steaks of wild-caught salmon
- ✓ 1medium white onion, peeled and sliced
- ✓ 2teaspoons minced garlic
- ✓ 1/2teaspoon salt
- ✓ 1/8teaspoon ground white pepper
- ✓ 1/2teaspoon dried dill weed
- ✓ 2tablespoons avocado oil
- ✓ 2tablespoons unsalted butter
- ✓ 2tablespoons lemon juice
- ✓ 1cup water

Directions:

➤ Place butter in a 4-quart slow cooker, then add salmon and drizzle with oil.

➤ Place remaining ingredients in a medium saucepan, stir until mixed and bring the mixture to boil over high heat.

➤ Then pour this mixture all over salmon and shut with lid.

➢ Plug in the slow cooker and cook salmon for 3 hours and 30 minutes at low heat setting or until salmon is tender.

➢ Serve straightaway.

Nutrition: Calories: 338 Fat: 11 g Protein: 13 g Carbs: 2.8 g Fiber: 7 g Sugar: 1.2 g

Lemon Pepper Tilapia

Preparation Time: 5 minutes

Cooking Time: 3 hours

Servings: 6

Ingredients:

- ✓ 6 wild-caught Tilapia fillets
- ✓ 4teaspoons lemon-pepper seasoning, divided
- ✓ 6tablespoons unsalted butter, divided
- ✓ 1/2cup lemon juice, fresh

Directions:

➤ Cut a large piece of aluminum foil for each fillet and then arrange them on a clean working space.

➤ Place each fillet in the middle of the foil, then season with lemon-pepper seasoning, drizzle with lemon juice and top with 1 tablespoon butter.

➤ Gently crimp the edges of foil to form a packet and place it into a 6-quart slow cooker.

➤ Plug in the slow cooker, shut with lid and cook for 3 hours at high heat setting or until cooked through. When done, carefully remove packets from the slow cooker and open the crimped edges and check the fish, it should be tender and flaky.

➤ **Nutrition: Calories: 321 Fat: 10 g Protein: 21 g Carbs: 1.2 g Fiber: 7 g Sugar: 1.8 g**

Clam Chowder

Preparation Time: 5 minutes

Cooking Time: 6 hours

Servings: 6

Ingredients:

- ✓ 20-ounce wild-caught baby clams, with juice
- ✓ 1/2cup chopped scallion
- ✓ 1/2cup chopped celery
- ✓ 1teaspoon salt
- ✓ 1teaspoon ground black pepper
- ✓ 1teaspoon dried thyme
- ✓ 1tablespoon avocado oil
- ✓ 2cups coconut cream, full-fat
- ✓ 2cups chicken broth

Directions:

- ➢ Grease a 6-quart slow cooker with oil, then add ingredients and stir until mixed.
- ➢ Plug in the slow cooker, shut with lid and cook for 4 to 6 hours at low heat setting or until cooked through.
- ➢ Serve straightaway.

Nutrition: Calories: 190 Fat: 14 g Protein: 12 g Carbs: 4.1 g Fiber: 17 g Sugar: 3.9 g

Soy-Ginger Steamed Pompano

Preparation Time: 5 minutes

Cooking Time: 1 hour

Servings: 6

Ingredients:

- ✓ 1wild-caught whole pompano, gutted and scaled
- ✓ 1bunch scallion, diced
- ✓ 1 bunch cilantro, chopped
- ✓ 3teaspoons minced garlic
- ✓ 1tablespoon grated ginger
- ✓ 1tablespoon swerve sweetener
- ✓ 1/4cup soy sauce; 1/4 cup white wine
- ✓ 1/4 cup sesame oil

Directions:

- ➤ Place scallions in a 6-quart slow cooker and top with fish.
- ➤ Whisk together remaining ingredients, except for cilantro, and pour the mixture all over the fish.
- ➤ Plug in the slow cooker, shut with lid and cook for 1 hour at high heat setting or until cooked through.
- ➤ Garnish with cilantro and serve.

Nutrition: Calories: 129 Fat: 13 g Protein: 18 g Carbs: 4 g Fiber: 17 g Sugar: 3.1 g

Vietnamese Braised Catfish

Preparation Time: 5 minutes

Cooking Time: 6 hours

Servings: 3

Ingredients:

- ✓ 1fillet of wild-caught catfish, cut into bite-size pieces
- ✓ 1scallion, chopped; 3red chilies, chopped
- ✓ 1tablespoon grated ginger
- ✓ 1/2cup swerve sweetener
- ✓ 2tablespoons avocado oil
- ✓ 1/4cup fish sauce, unsweetened

Directions:

- ➤ Place a small saucepan over medium heat, add sweetener and cook until it melts.
- ➤ Then add scallion, chilies, ginger and fish sauce and stir until mixed.
- ➤ Transfer this mixture in a 4-quart slow cooker, add fish and toss until coated.
- ➤ Plug in the slow cooker, shut with lid and cook for 6 hours at low heat setting until cooked.
- ➤ Drizzle with avocado oil and serve straightaway.

Nutrition: Calories: 156 Fat: 21 g Protein: 19 g Carbs: 0.2 g Fiber: 17 g Sugar: 0.1 g

Chili Prawns

Preparation Time: 5 minutes

Cooking Time: 1 hour

Servings: 6

Ingredients:

- ✓ 18-ounce wild-caught prawns, shell-on
- ✓ 1/2cup sliced scallions
- ✓ 1thumb-sized ginger, minced
- ✓ 1bulb. of garlic, peeled and minced
- ✓ 1tablespoon swerve sweetener
- ✓ 2tablespoons apple cider vinegar
- ✓ 2tablespoons Sambal Oelek
- ✓ 1tablespoon fish sauce, unsweetened
- ✓ 4tablespoons sesame oil
- ✓ 1/2cup tomato ketchup, keto and unsweetened
- ✓ 1egg, beaten

Directions:

- ➤ Place all the ingredients, except for prawns, oil, and egg in a 6-quart slow cooker and stir until mixed.
- ➤ Plug in the slow cooker, shut with lid and cook for 1 hour at high heat setting.

➢ Then add prawns and continue cooking for 15 minutes at high heat setting or until prawns turn pink.

➢ Stir in oil and egg and cook for 10 minutes.

➢ Drizzle with more fish sauce and serve.

Nutrition: Calories: 154 Fat: 13 g Protein: 15 g Carbs: 3.6 g Fiber: 17 g Sugar: 1.7 g

Tuna Salpicao

Preparation Time: 5 minutes

Cooking Time: 3 hours

Servings: 2

Ingredients:

- ✓ 8ounce cooked wild-caught tuna, cut into inch cubes
- ✓ 4jalapeno peppers, chopped
- ✓ 5red chili, chopped
- ✓ 1bulb. of garlic, peeled and minced
- ✓ 1teaspoon salt
- ✓ 1teaspoon ground black pepper
- ✓ 1cup avocado oil

Directions:

- ➢ Place all the ingredients except for tuna in a 4-quart slow cooker and stir until mixed.
- ➢ Plug in the slow cooker, shut with lid and cook for 4 hours at low heat setting.
- ➢ Then add tuna and continue cooking for 10 minutes at high heat setting.
- ➢ Serve straightaway.

Nutrition: Calories: 154 Fat: 13 g Protein: 15 g Carbs: 1.8 g Fiber: 17 g Sugar: 1.0 g

Soy-Ginger Braised Squid

Preparation Time: 5 minutes

Cooking Time: 8 hours

Servings: 6

Ingredients:

- ✓ 18-ounce wild-caught squid, cut into rings
- ✓ 2scallions, chopped
- ✓ 2bay leaves
- ✓ 1tablespoon grated ginger
- ✓ 1bulb. of garlic, peeled and minced
- ✓ 1/2cup swerve sweetener
- ✓ 1/4cup soy sauce
- ✓ 1/4cup oyster sauce
- ✓ 1/4cup avocado oil
- ✓ 1/4cup white wine

Directions:

- ➤ Plug in a 6-quart slow cooker, add all the ingredients and stir until mixed.
- ➤ Shut with lid and cook for 8 hours at low heat setting or until cooked through.
- ➤ Serve straightaway.

Nutrition: Calories: 154 Fat: 13 g Protein: 15 g Carbs: 3.4 g Fiber: 17 g Sugar: 1.9 g

Sea Bass in Coconut Cream Sauce

Preparation Time: 5 minutes

Cooking Time: 1 hour

Servings: 3

Ingredients:

- ✓ 18-ounce wild-caught sea bass
- ✓ 5jalapeno peppers
- ✓ 4stalks of bock Choy
- ✓ 2stalks of scallions, sliced
- ✓ 1tablespoon grated ginger
- ✓ 11/2 teaspoon salt
- ✓ 1tablespoon fish sauce, unsweetened
- ✓ 2cups coconut cream

Directions:

- ➢ Stir together all the ingredients except for bok choy and fish in a bowl and add this mixture in a 6-quarts slow cooker.
- ➢ Plug in the slow cooker, then add fish, top with bok choy and shut with lid.
- ➢ Cook sea bass for 1 hour and 30 minutes or until cooked.
- ➢ Serve straightaway.

Nutrition: Calories: 315 Fat: 17 g Protein: 15 g Carbs: 2.4 g Fiber: 17 g Sugar: 3.2 g

Beef & Pumpkin Stew

Preparation Time: 5 minutes

Cooking Time: 4 hours

Servings: 4

Ingredients:

- ✓ Teaspoon sage
- ✓ teaspoon mixed herbs
- ✓ Tablespoons rosemary
- ✓ Tablespoons thyme
- ✓ 6 tablespoons coconut oil
- ✓ 200g pumpkin
- ✓ 300g stewing steak
- ✓ Salt & pepper, to taste

Directions:

- ➢ Trim off every excess fat from the stewing steak, then transfer it into the crockpot.
- ➢ Season the steak with half of the coconut oil then and in the salt & pepper.
- ➢ Cover the crockpot, then cook on high setting for 1 hour.
- ➢ Remove the steak from the crockpot to a serving platter alongside all the remaining seasoning and coconut oil.

➢ Mix everything, then transfer back into the crockpot with the pumpkin and cook for 3 hours on a low setting.

➢ Serve with fresh mixed herbs and enjoy.

Nutrition: Calories: 324 Carbs: 3.7gFat: 11g Protein: 23g

Pepper Jalapeno Low Carb Soup

Preparation Time: 10 minutes

Cooking Time: 7 hours

Servings: 8

Ingredients:

- ➢ 1/4 teaspoon Paprika
- ➢ 1/2 teaspoon Pepper
- ➢ 1/2 chopped onion
- ➢ 1/2 teaspoon Xanthan gum
- ➢ 1/2 chopped green pepper
- ➢ 1/2 cup heavy whipping cream
- ➢ 1/2 lb. Cooked & crumbled bacon
- ➢ 3/4 cup cheddar cheese
- ➢ 3/4 cup Monterrey jack cheese
- ➢ teaspoon Salt
- ➢ 1 teaspoon Cumin
- ➢ 1 & 1/2-pounds chicken breasts, boneless
- ➢ Minced garlic cloves
- ➢ Seeded & chopped jalapenos
- ➢ 1tbsp. Butter
- ➢ 3 cups chicken broth
- ➢ Oz. Cream cheese

Directions:

➢ Dissolve the butter, then cook the green peppers, seasoning, jalapenos, and onions until translucent in a medium-sized pan.

➢ Scoop the mixture into the crockpot, then add in the chicken broth and breast.

➢ Cover the crockpot, then cook for 3-4 hours on high or 6-7 hours on a low setting.

➢ Separate the chicken, and shred it, then return it into the crockpot.

➢ Put in the heavy whipping cream, cream cheese, remaining cheeses, bacon, then stir until the cheese melts.

➢ Sprinkle the soup with xanthan gum to thicken, then allow it to simmer uncovered on low for 10 minutes.

➢ Serve, then top with cheddar cheese, bacon, or jalapenos and enjoy.

Nutrition: Calories: 240 Carbs: 1g Fat: 20g Protein: 11g

Lean Beef & Mixed Veggies Soup

Preparation Time: 8 minutes

Cooking Time: 6 hours

Servings: 6

Ingredients:

- ➢ 1/2 teaspoon Garlic salt, if desired
- ➢ Peeled small onion
- ➢ 1 diced small green pepper
- ➢ 1 teaspoon Garlic & herb seasoning
- ➢ 1 small zucchini, sliced into rounds
- ➢ 1 can of rinsed & drained cannellini beans
- ➢ 1 small yellow squash, sliced into rounds
- ➢ 1 (14 1/2 ounces) can diced roasted tomatoes
- ➢ 1 & 1/2-pounds beef stew meat
- ➢ 1-2 teaspoon Ground pepper
- ➢ 1-3 bay leaves
- ➢ Cups of frozen mixed vegetables
- ➢ Cups low salt beef broth
- ➢ Peeled & chopped garlic cloves

Directions:

- ➢ Add all the ingredients except the zucchini cannellini beans, mixed vegetables, and yellow squash into the crockpot.
- ➢ Cover the pot, then cook on high for 4 hours.

➤ After 4 hours, add in the zucchini, cannellini beans, yellow squash, and mixed vegetables.

➤ Season to taste, and cook for an extra 2 hours on high.

➤ Once done, stir, then serve and enjoy.

Nutrition: Calories: 50 Carbs: 1g Fat: 0g Protein: 2g

Lightning Source UK Ltd.
Milton Keynes UK
UKHW050151170621
385583UK00015B/251

9 781803 113609